1960s Racing Car

Viking Longship

American Train

Spy Plane

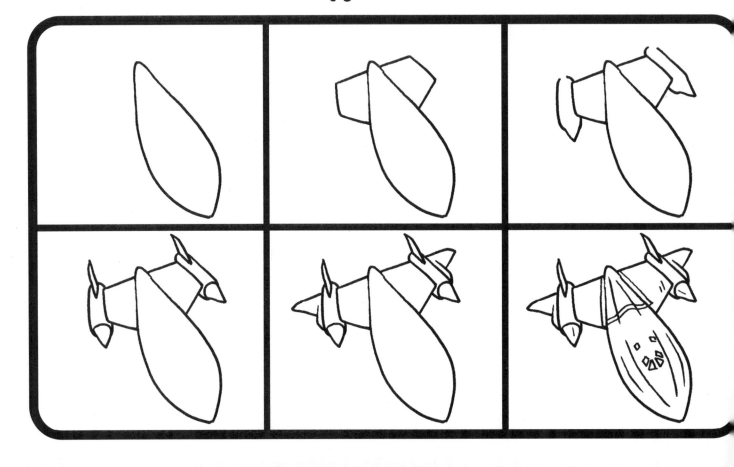

Formula 1 Racing car

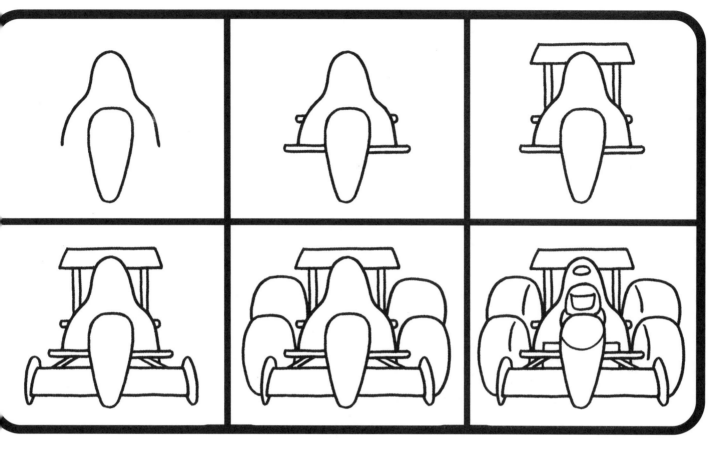

Road Roller

Cruise Ship

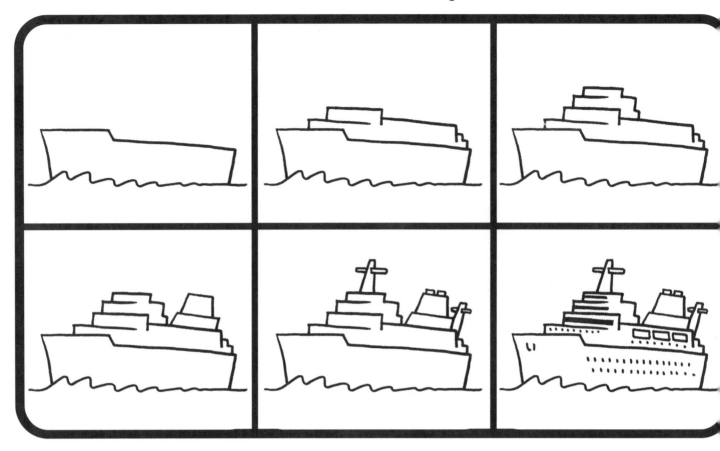

Chopper Bike

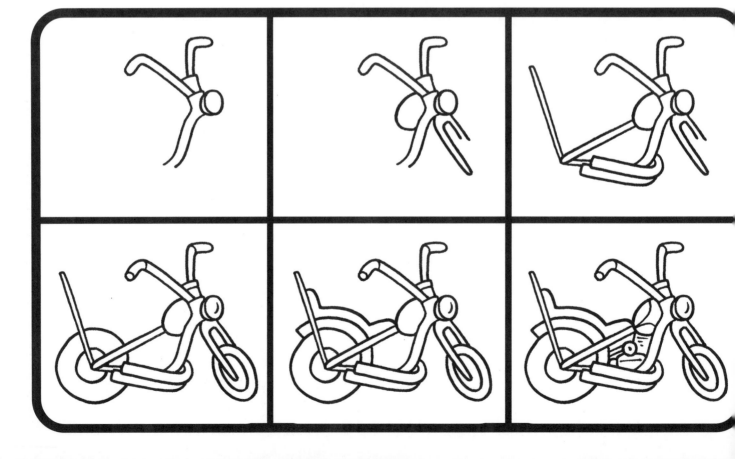

747 Jumbo Jet

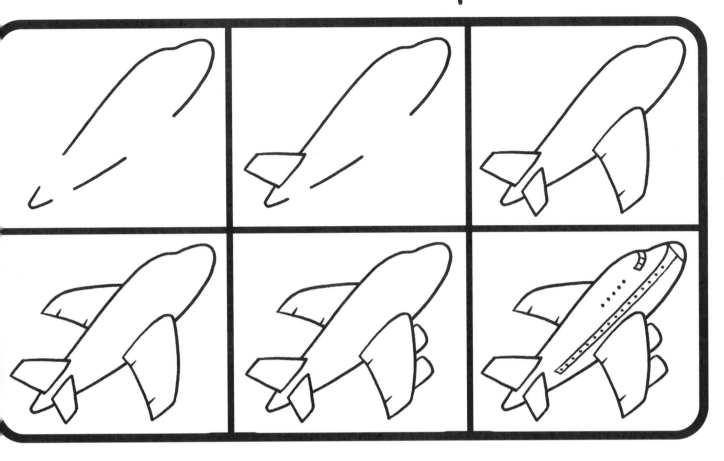

custom car

Mini

Digger

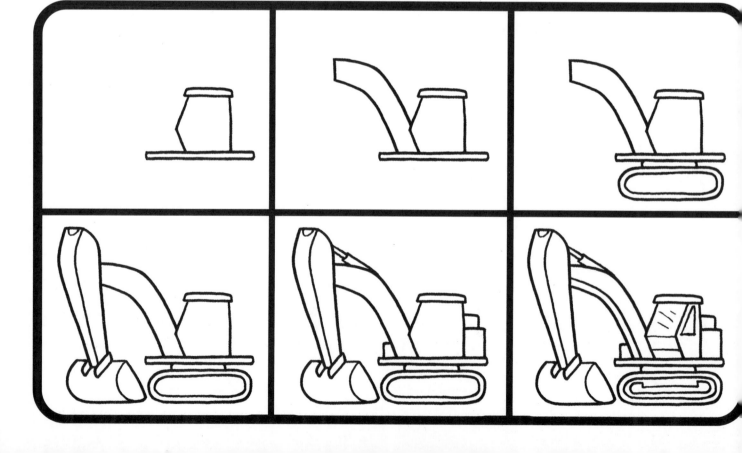

Lifeboat

Helicopter

Ski-Doo

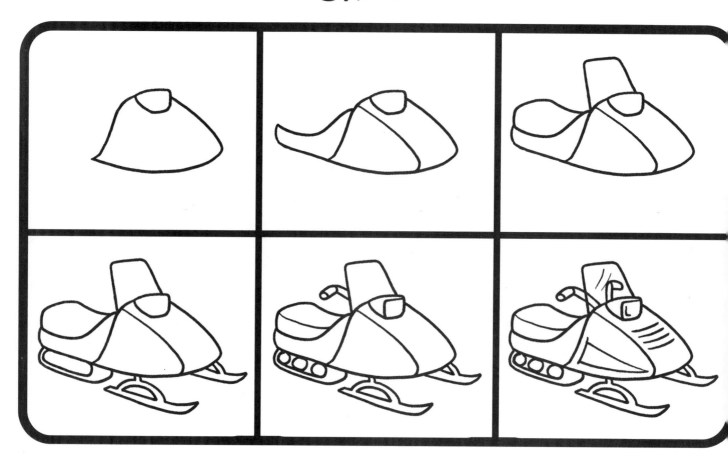

Moon Buggy

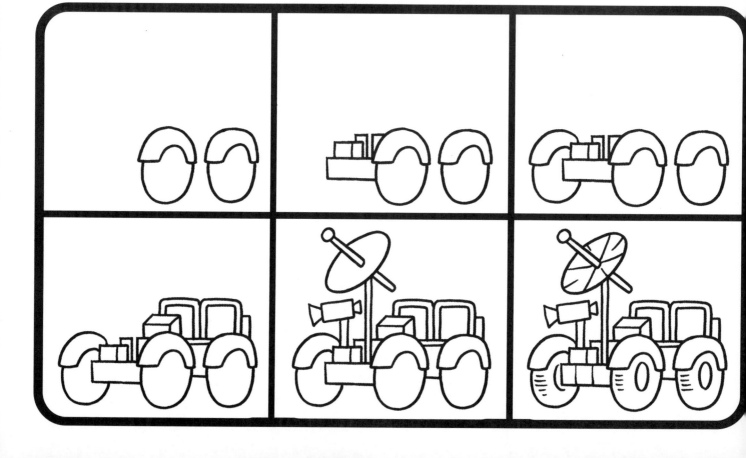

Crane

TGV Train

Combine Harvester

Racing Motorbike

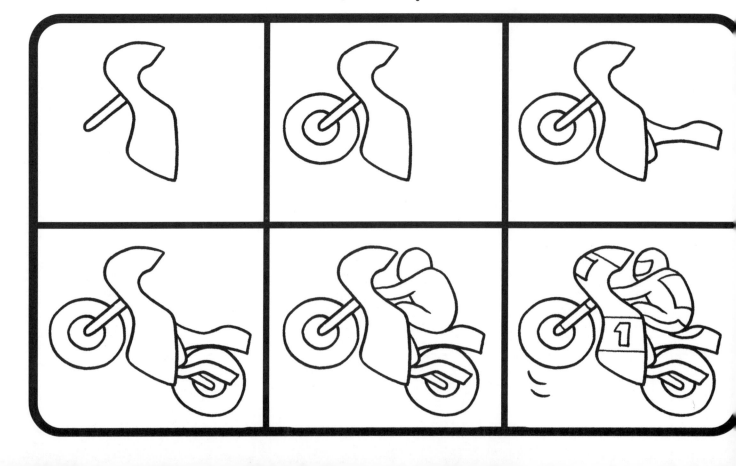

Police car

Wright Brothers' Flyer

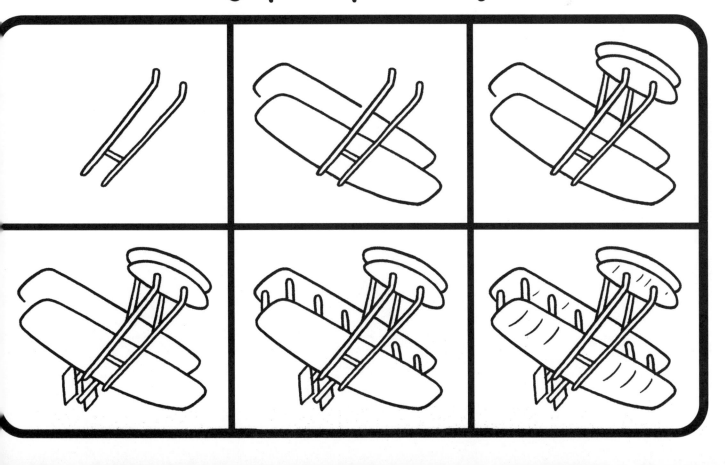

Mini Digger

Jet Ski

Space Shuttle

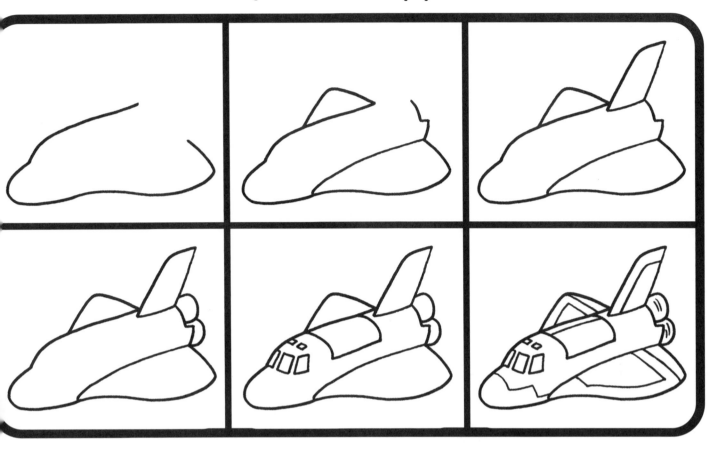

Chinese Junk Ship

Land Rover

Bullet Train

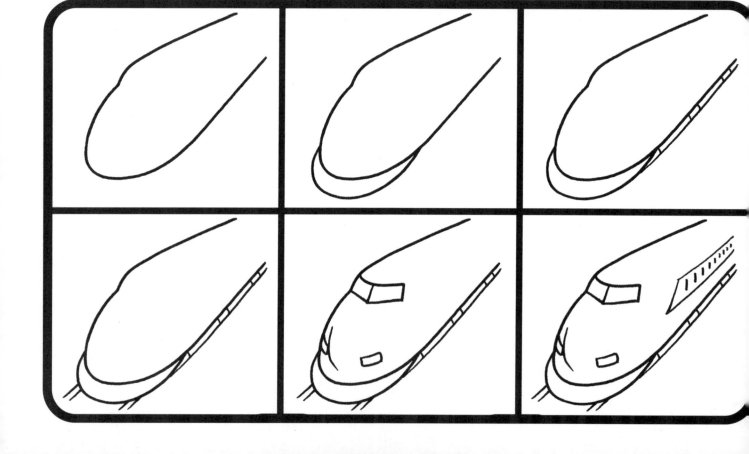

Motocross Bike

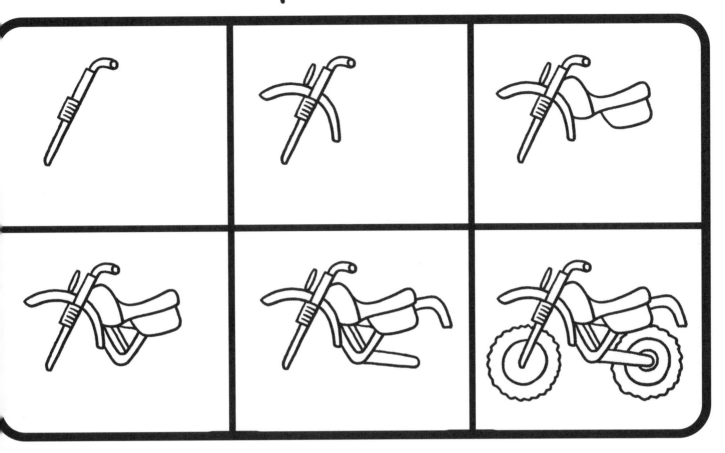

Traction Engine

Stealth Fighter

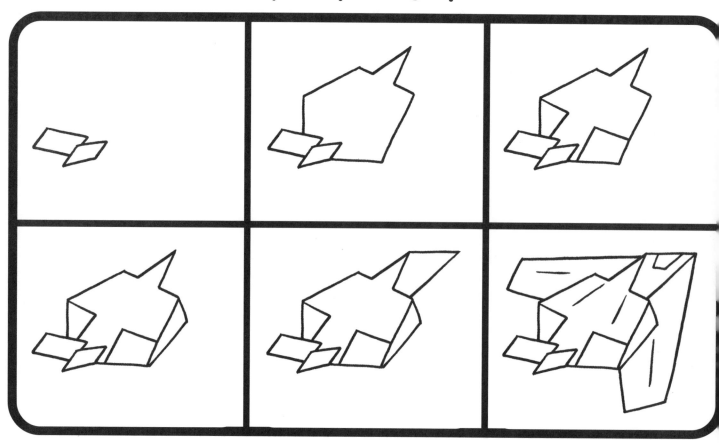

The first car

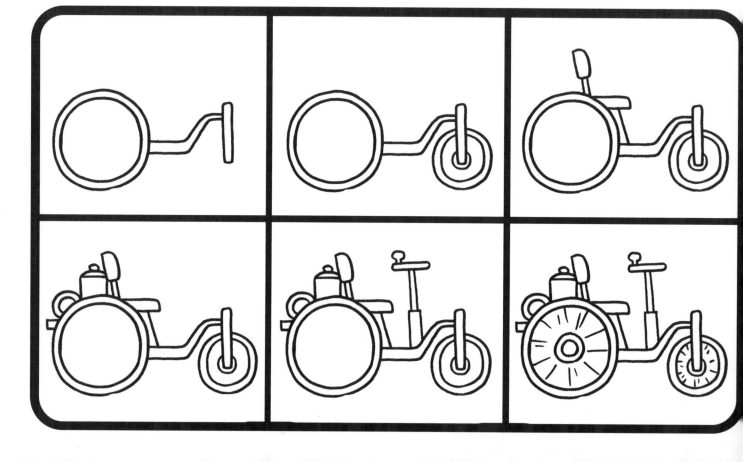

Dumper

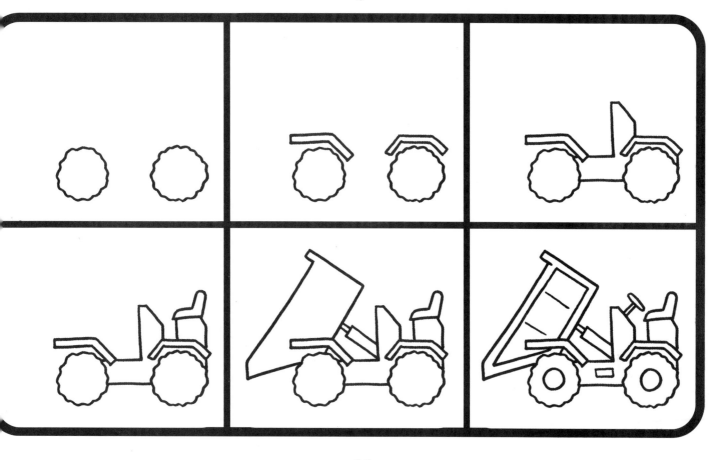

Cadillac

Motorised Rickshaw

Hydro-foil

Snow Plough Engine

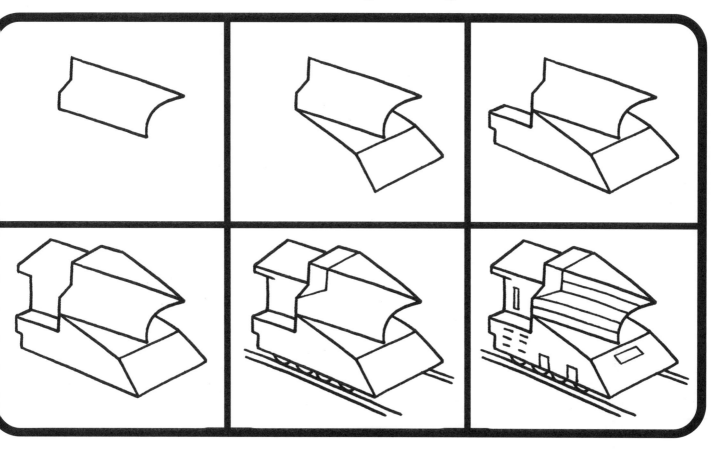

Spitfire

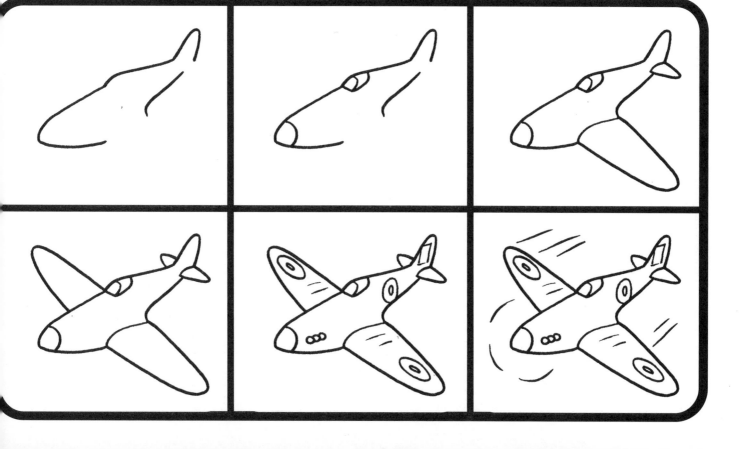

Bubble Car

Cement Truck

Microlight

Paddle Steamer

17th Century Ship

Monster Truck

Dumper Truck

Scooter

Le Mans Racing car

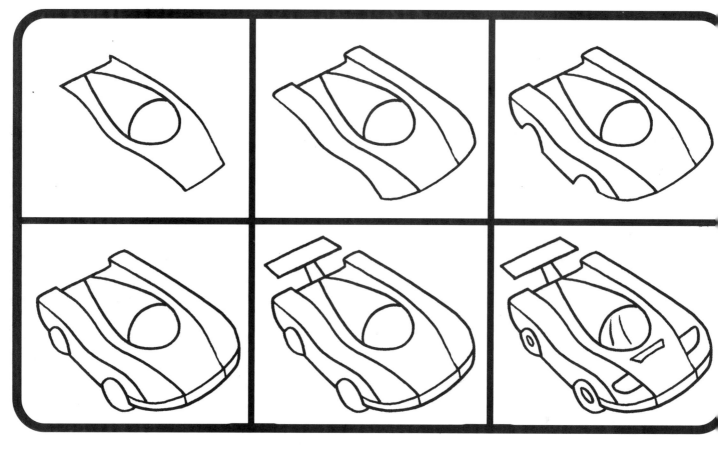

Skip Truck

Hovercraft

The Mallard Train

Roller

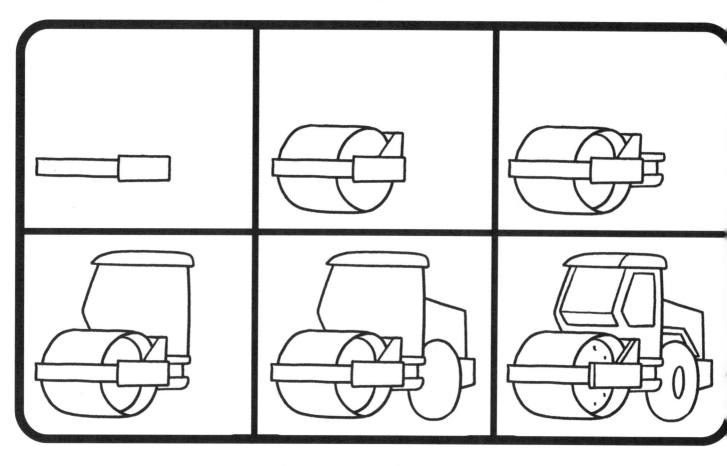

Fishing Boat

Pick-up Truck

Lorry

Speed Boat

1901 Oldsmobile

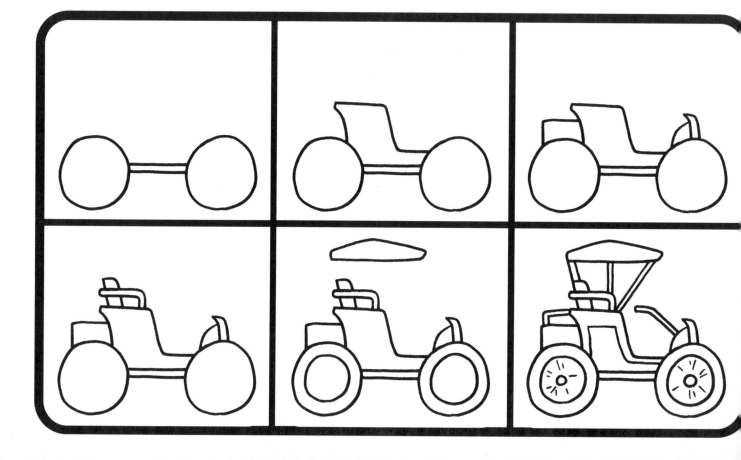

Sea Plane

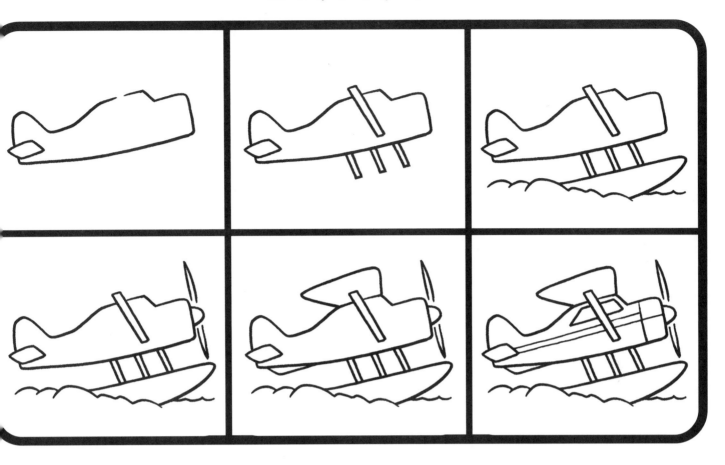

London Bus

Tractor

Snow cat

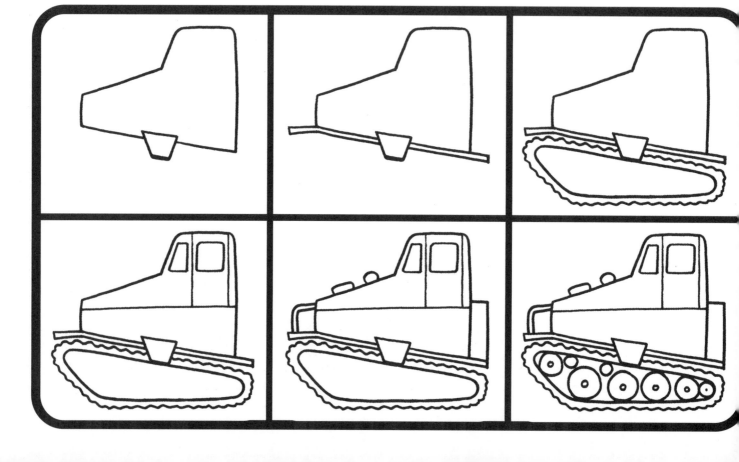

Fire Engine

Stock car

Thrust II

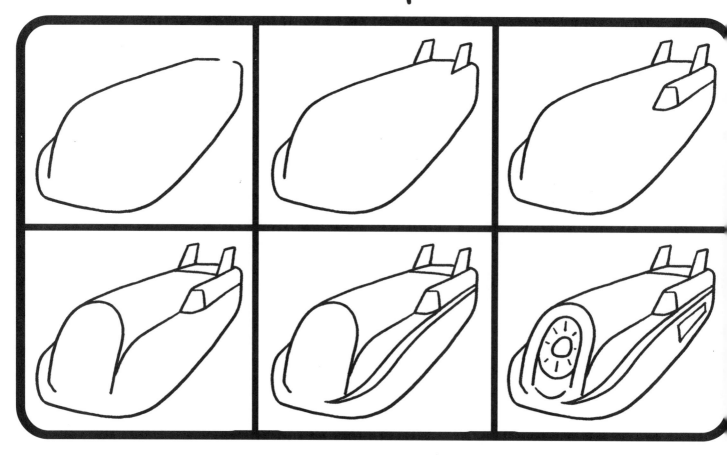

Tug Boat

The Rocket

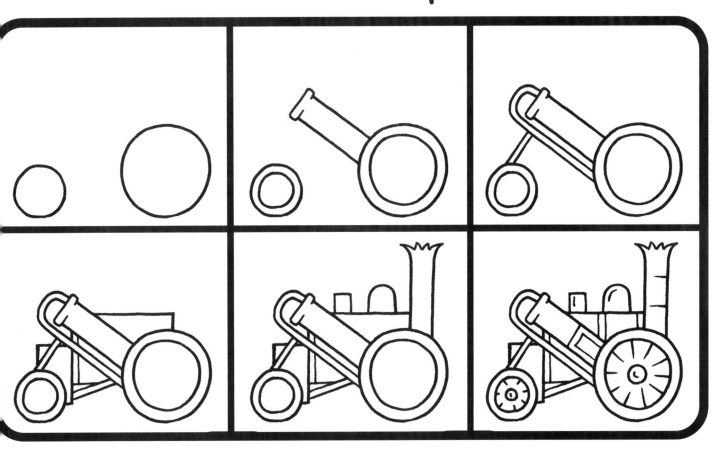

citroen 2CV

Quad Bike

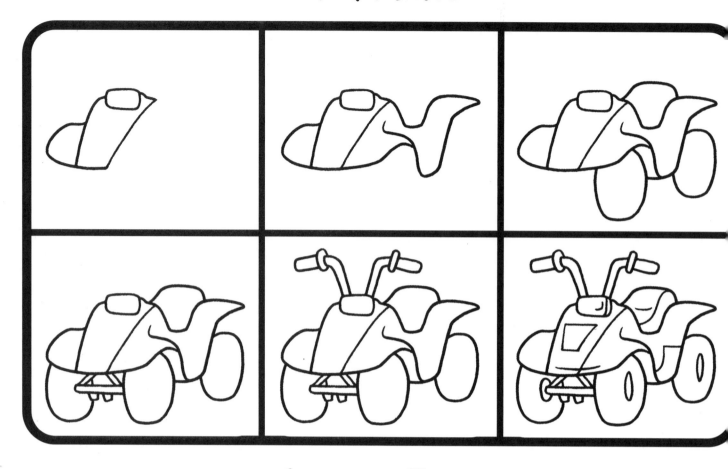

London Taxi

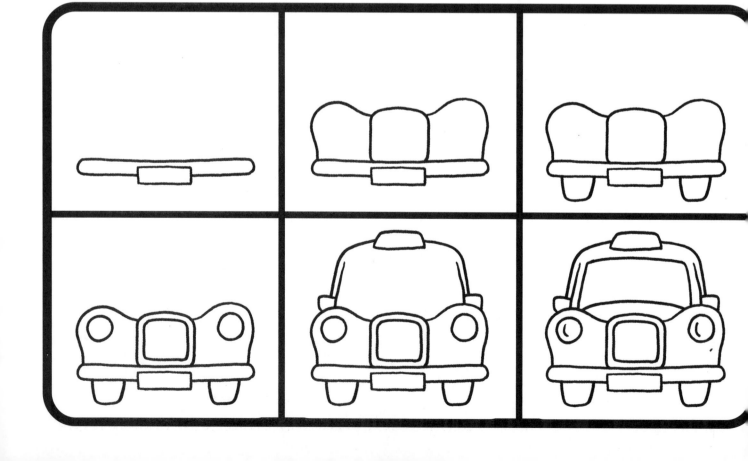

Coach

Submersible

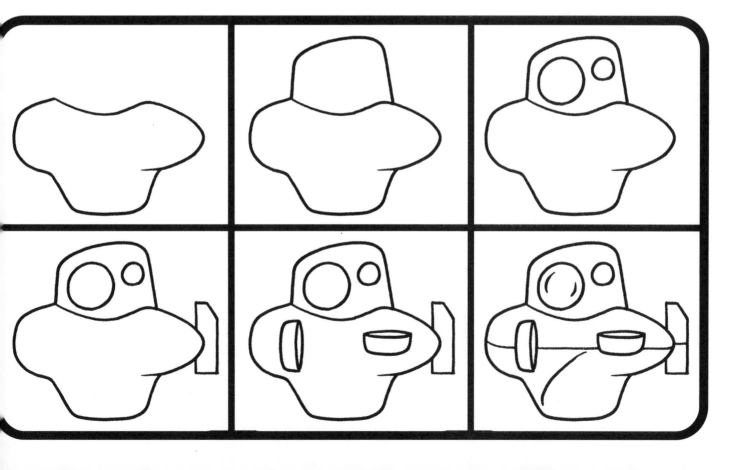

1920s Motorbike

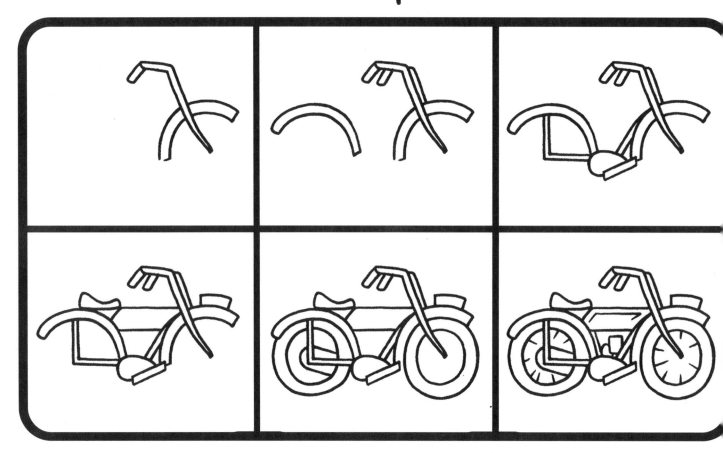

Concept Electric Car

Bulldozer

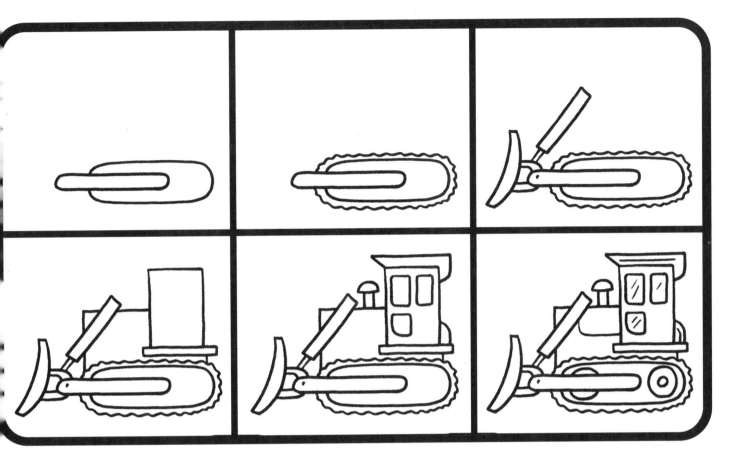

4x4 Off-Road Vehicle

Rolls Royce

Light Aircraft

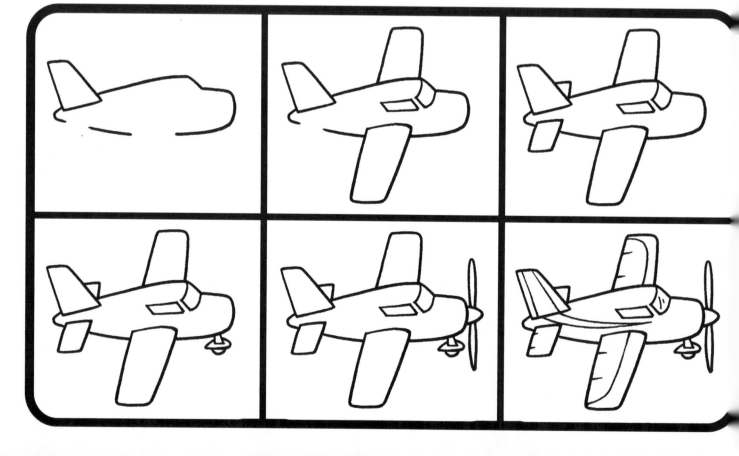

Dragster

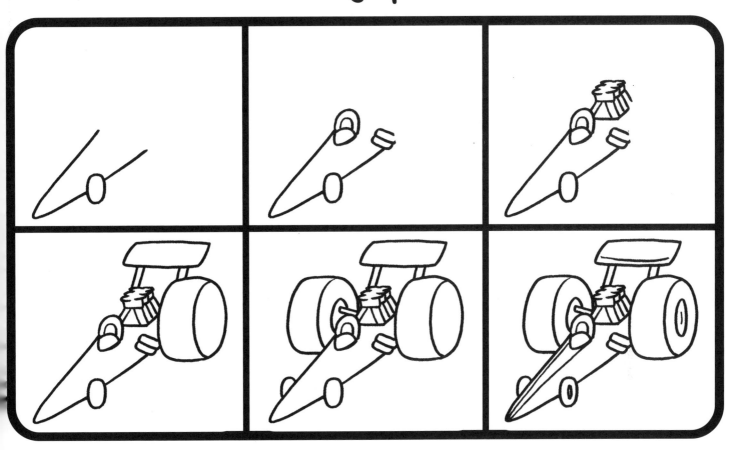

Wild West Train

Model T ford

Dune Buggy

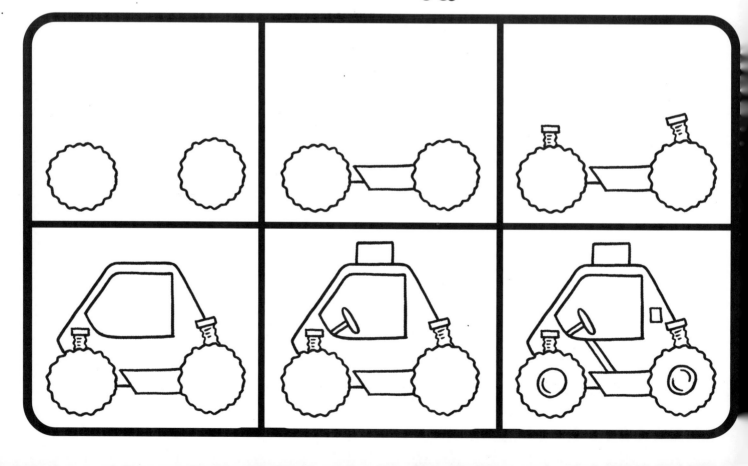

Gossamer Albatross

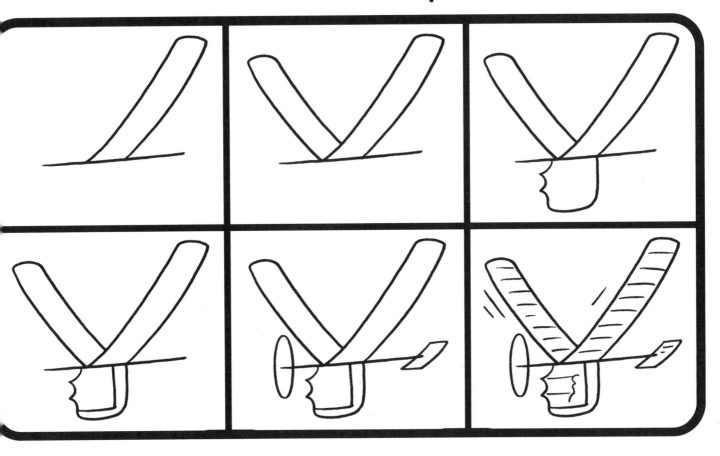

Fork Lift Truck

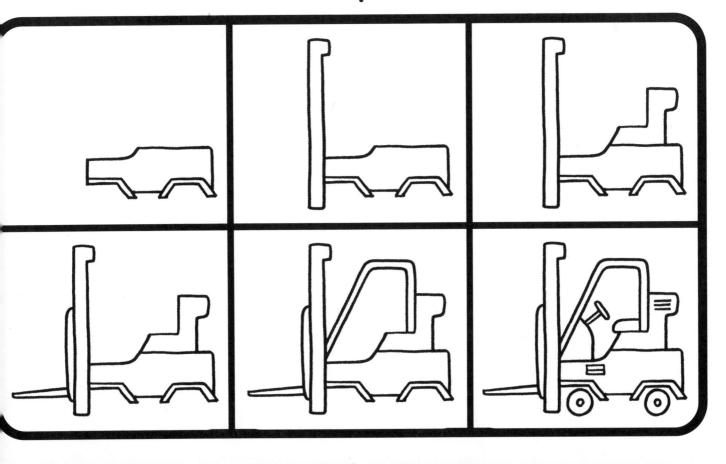

Concorde

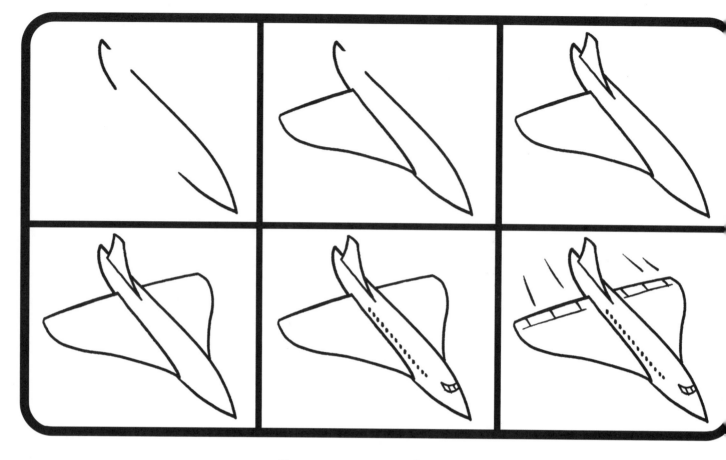

Stretch Limo

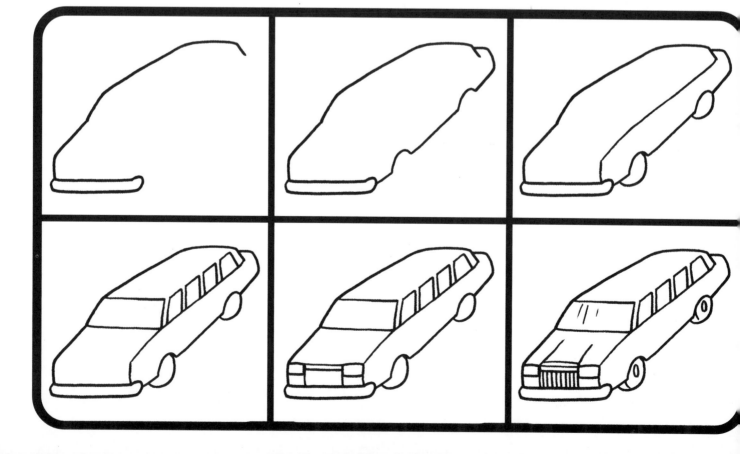

Yacht

Jeep

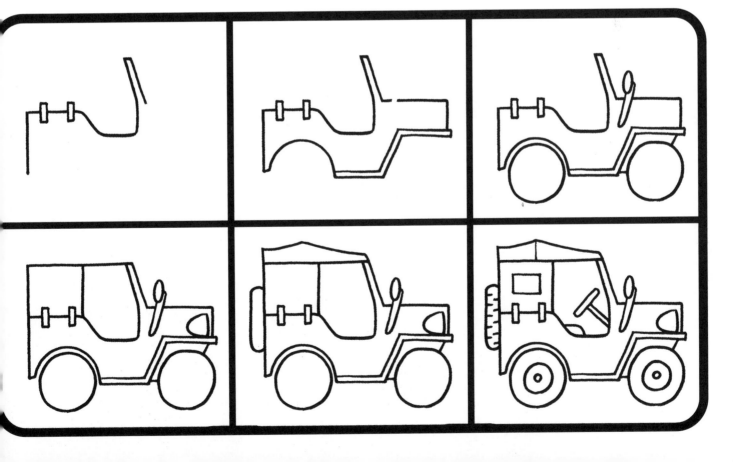

Submarine

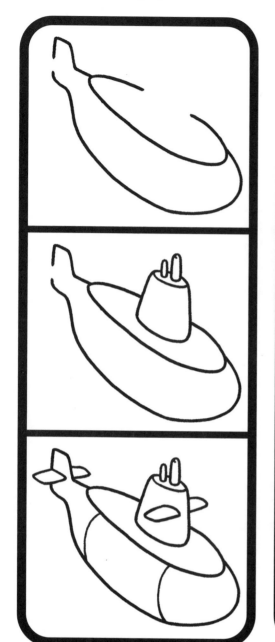

Bi-Plane

Monorail Train

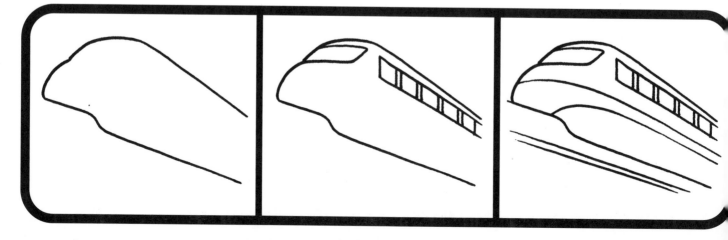

cable car

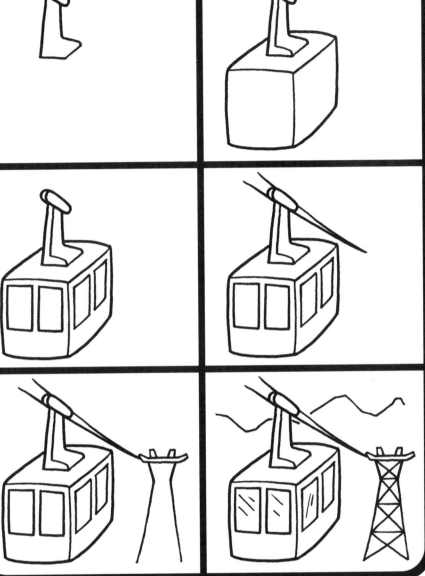

Sunray

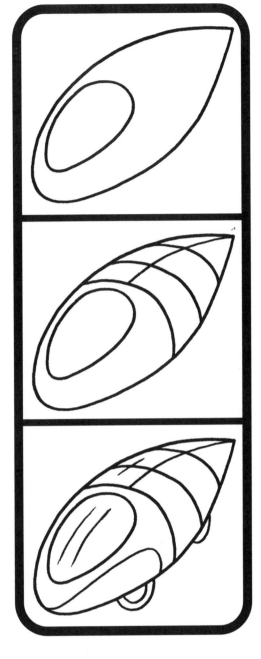

Airship

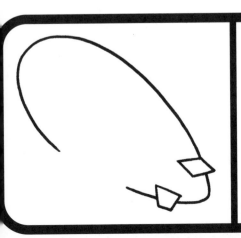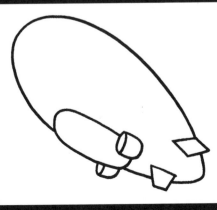

VW Beetle

Transit Van

Hang-glider

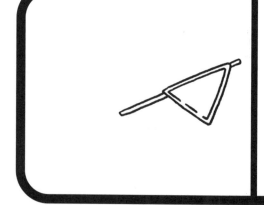

funicular

Rocket

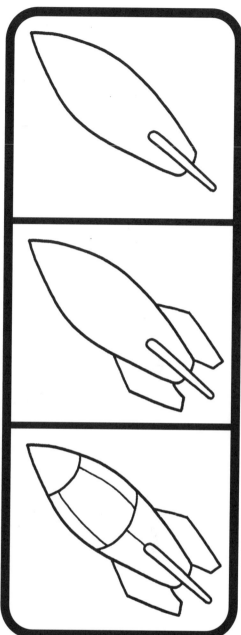

Lindbergh's 'Spirit of St Louis'

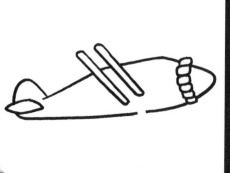  

Glider

Tram

Bell X-1 Rocket

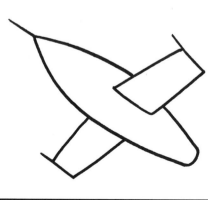